MW01199387

Bexley
July 2019

For Kathy —
In admiration and
gratitude for your work —

XO Amy

THE MIRACLES

AMY LEMMON

C&R Press
Conscious & Responsible

THE MIRACLES

For my children: two miracles

TABLE OF CONTENTS

Prelude

The Miracles

Blessed be the Lord; who worked a miracle of unfailing love for me when I was in
sore straits (like a city besieged)
                    —Psalm 31:21

I.

We took our firstborn to the Cloisters, his first Easter.
You photographed me holding him in the Medieval
herb garden based on *millefleurs* tapestries,
gray skies, diffuse light, my new linen outfit loose

on my loose new mother's body. The baby's eyes
looked ancient, peering out below his little blue hat.
I do not know who was saved on that cold Easter,
only that the baby's grandmother exhibited

towards him the kind of raw adoration
given the Messiah by the humble shepherds
and their sheep. I thought I wanted to be a mother.
It was too late to change my mind.

I wanted to be home lying down, listening
to medieval chant and polyphony by Anonymous 4.
Green grow'th the holly….so doth the ivy
The garden was only a little green that day,

though in a matter of weeks the new shoots
would push up, the everyday miracle
of the growth cycle helped along by
the world's best horticultural curators.

We can believe something is always growing,
something else dying, and even in growth death
is contained, blah blah, O the cycle, the DNA,
the damnable incessant blank life force.

The baby boy reposes unimpressed
in Mother's arms, blinks at his dominion's
dull glare, admits no distractions from his business—
to see and own it all, seen and unseen.

II.

The clowns in the pediatric surgical suite
waiting room were two smallish women, chipper
in white makeup. One played ukulele.
Star light, star bright, heads tilted together

to find their harmony. They didn't know
our daughter's name was Stella, meaning star,
or that we were waiting for them to take her,
put her to sleep, cut open her chest

and fix her heart with Gore-Tex®, a miracle fiber
that would live in her body the rest of her life
after healthy tissue had grown over it, closing the hole
she was mistakenly born with. Stella was hungry, didn't get

why she couldn't nurse. She was hungry, dammit, could smell
the milk I would have to pump while she was in surgery.
Nine months old, the same time outside
as she'd been inside, still my body's job to feed her.

In certain religions clowning is a ritual to avert evil,
deflecting demonic attention from serious religious activities.
These clowns found us in our little hiding place though
I didn't want us to be found, I wanted to cry alone

like you did when you vanished to the restroom,
left me with my hungry crying baby who could not understand
why Mother didn't feed her, who never gave up
not even when we might have wished she would.

The wait was longer than we had been told,
the lights brighter than seemed necessary,
families unnaturally jolly with their sick children.
The scene shrank to her cries, your reddened eyes.

III.

When I get to the kitchen she's already dancing,
boogeying down to the radio—*Here's one
from nine-teen-six-ty-four*—we barely get reception
but by some miracle Rhythm Review is loud and clear

on WBGO out of Newark, New Jersey.
I grab her hands and start to twist, and when we insist
her brother puts down his shiny handheld game
and joins us on the stained linoleum.

Stella works her little mojo for all its worth,
tiny features all a-beam, soft arms and legs
barely under control. Next up is Smokey Robinson,
"Tears of a Clown," that old American song I never fully got

till I heard the English Beat's version—Ranking Roger
singing *clone* for *clown*—in 1984, I edged my off-white
knock-off Keds closer to the boy (skanking, soaked
white-shirted back) I wanted the way I wanted

patty melts or more beer—the cut just two and a half minutes,
so short you'd almost miss it before the next track, "Rough
Rider," a hundred quavers slower and a lot less sweat.
I had not yet learned that wanting makes nothing so.

I had not yet found and lost you. I lose myself
in anamnesis, kinesis, pure pleasure of musculature,
three bodies moving, mine plus two my body
once contained, And this cruddy Queens kitchen

swirls into solid gold thanks to Felix Hernandez,
the Maestro of the Groove, Smokey singing with his Miracles
to a circus of flute and bassoon and hey, I'm dancing,
I'm dancing right here, right now, with mine.

11

Fugue

M23

9/11/01

As we stood at the intersection of Bloomie Nails
and Everything Bagels, the crosstown bus approached,
the only one running, calzone-stuffed and grunting.
In four weeks my daughter would slither wet on my belly,
turn blue until the nurse turned her pink and laid her
on my breast, warm, irretrievable. On the bus,
the bulge of her bought me a seat
between the Bajan nanny and the white-haired woman
whose appointment at St. Vincent's would have to be
rescheduled. We were bound for the East Side,
the Stuyvesant Town deli, a line desperate for ham
and cheese, minestrone, enormous water bottles. At my friend's
apartment, the TV gave the grainy story over and over.

Audacious: An Acrostic

Here she is: smiling and posed, hand on knee.
Oh where did she get that shirt? Tie-dyed
Pinks and purples swirl into a sparkle-studded heart
In the center of her chest, just above the scar
No one really notices anymore. Someone else
Gave her the sparkly shirt, dressed her in it just

For Picture Day (which I somehow missed). And thank God
Or she would have been in the drab uniform her principal
Requires even of the kids in District 75, the *special* ones.

Could it be that mothering her will always be a series of
Handings-over, letting others more qualified tend, evaluate,
And teach? Who will walk with her when she turns 21 if there's
Not a drop left in the well? What kind of woman will she be—this
Girl who's never heeded *No?* May her cherry chapstick kisses
Ever find a gentle cheek, all her bedtime stories end with *Best Beloved*.

After Bathing I Smell Smoke

after Galway Kinnell

For I can rattle the pans while cooking,
drop a dish or run the vacuum in the hallway
and Stella will stay behind her shut door, sleeping
or drawing, reading or tending her kennel of stuffed dogs,
but let me run the water and swirl in Epsom salts
and lavender oil, slide in with a book and coffee
or just recline and soak, eyes closed,
reading my own thoughts as they skein out,
twining like one of those interlocking
wind sculptures gently rotating on a breeze,
and she will dash to my room, root out everything most
threatening to our mutual safety and tranquility
and, as I rise dripping to reach for the towel,
she is pilfering my most secret journal and scrawling
stick figures on its pages with my hidden permanent markers,
removing every knife and pair of scissors from their secure places.

After I have dressed, chased her from my bed, retrieved
my vintage edition of *Through the Looking Glass*,
I smell it, something burning or just burnt,
and on the one uncovered patch of parquet
I see a wooden match half-blackened, and after sniffing
every corner and pile—papers, folders, books,
clothing waiting to be ignited—satisfied that no spark waits to flame
into the heat of our destruction, I take the dead match
and say *No NO, never never NEVER play with matches!*
and collapse my arms around her small solid fireplug body,
which softens as she murmurs *Sorry, so sorry, Mom,*
into my shoulder, and I pray that this innocence
will not be her downfall, blessing her every hair,
the animal scent of her bowed head.

Errant Pastoral

Midwestern summers of my youth sprawled,
protracted and stifling. How many days
did I while away gazing at clouds,
at blue sky through green leaves? How many
nights longing for something I did not know
I was missing? None of the scraped Volkswagens
or blunt Gremlins rumbling past were yours,
no puff of escaped smoke. Now, two children
later, grass prickles and crawls, threat
of creeping things bearing sicknesses. Meadow
weeds give way to the occasional cow,
maples outgrow their usefulness. Can I have
a do-over, another chance at pushing out
two separate creatures shading pink and blue?
I remember a Bach-washed room, a midwife—
mother to a supermodel—her Swedish cheekbones.
You took photos out the birthing room window:
the West Side perpetually under construction,
gray Hudson pulsing, taunt of the Palisades.
Lavender always conjures your massage the nights
I labored, my fields forever out of view.

Discontinued

When the boy finally cleaned his room, he found
a salad plate cracked in two, hidden who knows
how long. "Those dishes are twenty years old,"
I shrugged. "We need new ones anyway."

Our wedding pattern was called Athena, chosen
before I had a clue we'd live in a Greek
neighborhood, not stoneware or china,
but *porcelaine lumiere,* a fancy name for ceramic.

Music, I've read, enhances the taste of food.
Sweet tastes are linked with higher-pitched sounds,
while lower tones and brass evoke the savory
and the bitter. When the music stops,

I suppose, taste buds are on their own.
Bitterness in nature keeps us safe
from poisoning ourselves. Animals get it,
humans don't. We swallow bitter pills.

Our agreement was whoever cooked,
the other did the dishes. I do both now.
I never was that young wife in the olive oil
commercial, wasp-waisted, hair neatly pulled back

save a few tendrils attractively framing the face,
stirring something impossibly good and good for you
in a vintage bowl with a long wooden spoon,
feeding a family on plates that never shattered.

Good Housekeeping

Panic presents as children's bright paint fingered
onto white walls, a missing glass doorknob,
metal shaft stumped through, the lock awry.
I always lose things, splice orange halves on lemons.

No, I am not Doing Okay. The hallway
sputters teakettle-like, floors simmer with damage.
Elderly moldings crumble like stale scones.
The silver tea service blackens, a factory stack.

My great-grandmother's *Elizabeth Harding, Bride*,
the Procter & Gamble handbook for housewives,
instructed how to clean with Ivory Soap—
the walls, the floors, even the grand piano.

Gran used ammonia on windows, diluted,
didn't dare breathe. The house was her domain.
I inherited only the ghost, the guilt.
I put off taking out the trash for days.

Your friend I hired to babysit left messes
(*E. says she has depression,* our son told me).
After the accident, she *stopped by the hospital*
before relieving me so I could see you.

You never lived here but our home is emptied—
ashes on the highboy, photo on the shelf.
We hated housework, fought it again and again,
no progress, no time off for good behavior.

The bathtub overflows—*voila!*—the floor
gets washed, but soon parquet tents and buckles.
I call the claims adjuster. The landlady frets.
A glass shatters—*poof*—the kitchen floor is spotless.

Two and a half bedrooms can rent as three.
They'll rent again as such when—if—we move.
No tenant leaves a place that's under market.
Insurance never covers what you think.

SEA-BANDS™

I got them first to navigate the waters
of pregnancy, so I could ride the subway
without gorge rising, without feeling faint.
Gray elasticized wrist bands with a white
plastic bead sewn into the middle to press
the acupressure point between the cords
on the underside of each wrist. Always wear both
or it won't work. Constant steady pressure
on the points will take away the stress response,
will take away the feeling and the fear of feeling.
I worry they identify me as fragile,
a wimpy woman prone to fainting spells
who carries smelling salts in her worn handbag.
The bands peek out from my sleeves,
not quite the same shade as my sweater,
not quite covered by bracelets. Evidence
of old wrist-slashings, I think—fragility *in extremis*,
giving in to the desire to give up entirely.
While I carried my children, the bands were badges
of some sort of honor, as if I needed
a reminder that my body's upheaval had purpose.
Now at forty thousand feet they are a godsend,
orienting me to myself, positioning
a part of me that can take good care,
that doesn't really need the beverage
service *Right Now* or free wifi, the part
that is grounded even a mile up
in the air, and up in the air
when flying is called for.

Animal Husbandry

Six months before we met you went vegetarian. I never
saw you eat anything with hooves or beaks, though
you powered through a Maine lobster (*Never again*, you said)
and for a time had a fondness for scallops.

Always overheated, you favored tank tops
your dad called *Guinea tees*. In midlife
we would be one hot pair, fanning each other
in crowds, cranking down the thermostat.

good run   good gravy
good grief   good genes

The Armsby Calorimeter was designed to measure
how much feed cows need to produce X amount
of milk or meat. It took up a whole brick building,
still standing on the campus of the Pennsylvania
State University, where nutritionists just discovered
that eating avocados and walnuts may lower bad cholesterol,
allowing me to feel only moderately bad after eating
another serving of Alumni Swirl
from the famous Creamery.

good fats   good measure
good mouthfeel   good egg

                  The vast expanse of summer days,
I am left with the care and feeding of our young,
who will make their own poor dietary choices,
saved, perhaps, by some fluke of engineering,
a passion for sport, keeping their upturned faces
shielded from the sun.

TRIBORO PHYSICAL THERAPY

Because it hangs the color of the sky,
the sign shouts everywhere. 24th Avenue
creaks along, salt-dusted sidewalks with thin dark patches.
Inside, a motto chides, *Never Ever Ever Give Up!*

My son sits in the waiting room, writing
information from the routine to the peculiar
on a standardized form. He texts:
Are you my primary care provider?

His phone dies. I hesitate: I could stop by
and check, but he must begin to handle things,
my guidance a wavering pole's refraction
in the rear-view mirror of his adulthood.

Eighteen years now of his body,
noticing its changes, his mind blooming,
all the dark processes I never had control over.
My son, my son, I have not forsaken you.

Jagged leaf from the father's tree,
spring loaded, he forges the plowed earth
of his intellect, turns jaggedly to veer
out of control like the handle that steers

this ridiculous metaphor to its inevitable halt.
Per instructions, the boy pulls the bar
down with both hands, then lets it rise
slowly, logging reps I cannot see.

What to Fix, What to Keep Broken

The doorknobs, don't get me started: antique glass
with brass hardware that's lost all practicality,
resistant to adjustments and tightening.
When our daughter locked herself in her room—
the knob fell out and she couldn't put it right—
I took the whole assembly off the door,
duct-taped the latch bolt flat
so it wouldn't catch again. I've given up
on the linen closet, just hid the inside
knob somewhere. It's good enough,
as is the short bathroom towel rack,
the only one now that the long one
won't stay up. I tucked it in the corner,
waiting for help. What else? I could go
metaphorical, all the promises and resolutions,
the intentions paving my brain's Merry Hell Road,
and of course my heart shattering over and over
in this place, beginning with you, measuring
the windows for custom blinds, installing them
and then sweating with me on the futon,
blinds down, *Privacy Please*, no one could see us
through the big picture window. You were the first
of so many to come and go, and now I guess
I'll let the damn thing stay broken,
since it seems useful enough this way,
and though I tried over and over,
I never could find the right screw
or wrench or patch to make it whole.

Miracles of Footwear

The shoes are paired
on the closet door rack.

The chromosomes are not.

one extra
        makes all
                the difference

        chiasma
            meiosis
                mitosis

                        asynapsis

failure: pairing
of homologous
chromosomes

For weeks the children
sleep head-to-foot
in the same bed.

I cross my legs
and uncross them.
My lap flattens.

I sleep with four pillows.
Now even your shoes
are gone—still
an imaginary closet
spills with your
abandoned finery.

Pursuit

Grief chases me around the house.
I fend it off with chocolate,
with cheese and crackers, with wine.
I fend it off with music,
but music makes it stronger,
especially that song,
you know the one.

I yell "BOO!" in its face to spook
it into a corner.
It explodes, laughing.
I spit at it and run away.

Grief doesn't follow at first,
creeps up slowly, seeming to glide.

Hello, Dear.
Soft breath warms my ear.
I let Grief take my hand

and then I am weeping again on its
shoulder, my oldest,
lumpiest pillow.

Riff – A

Our Measure of Misfortune

"This is it," I thought. A sun-breaking-through-clouds,
angel-chorus-washing-over thought. "Nothing else bad can happen
to us. Our parents won't sicken and die, no one we love
will get cancer, there won't be any bad accidents—"
Somehow my shocked mind concocted this lovely fiction,
palliative to the unimaginable horror we faced:
a *defective* child, *genetic abnormality*, the baby booby prize.

* * *

The train lurches and a woman sprawls to the floor.
The man she's with turns in the other direction.
"You almost killed me!" she screeches.
Other men rush to lift her to a seat. "You're difficult
to walk with," he says, hugging a pole mid-car.
Two busybodies cluck for half an hour,
volume turned up when the man gets off
at Times Square with the fallen woman.
"They *were* together!"   *cluck cluck.*
Where is the tenderness of late?
Where the privacy to choose your own destruction,
to love, to cleave to and from?

* * *

after Tintoretto

As your arm settles on the back of my chair,
dying sun graces the table, lighting my face.
The restaurant is suddenly transformed
into a Renaissance tableau.
Chairs perfectly arranged,
a hush lifts visibly
as I ascend.

Classic Vinyl

I swear to God, if I hear "American Pie"
one more time, decomposed grave-rot rank,
I'm firing off an email to the station. Present
and accounted for, that certain aural *ouch*
that comes the dozen-billionth time you've bitten your lip
in vain attempt to stave off a good cry

because *the music died* that day. Who wouldn't cry?
Who wouldn't bake his favorite apple pie
(true: not just cliché)? Crumbs on upper lip,
moustache or no. The wine he drank
and spilled—on the old rug, the futon couch,
the throw blanket—was red, of course, present

when he stopped to pay the toll, present
when they saw him fumble for his wallet, not cry-
ing even when he thought of the kids. I'll vouch-
safe no reply, no excuse, hire no spy.
Let his lawyer brother pull rank,
get colleagues to pro-bono spring him. A slip-

pery slope, no car, no work—no work, a blip
on the court's screen. *Plaintiff? Present.*
Whatever. Continue through the records, rank
and file. Points on the license for years, a cry
for help? At least he didn't hit a py-
lon or a person, crash a guard rail. *Ouch!*

Ouch! Ouch! Ouch! Ouch! sobs old Lear. *Ouch!*
the rapidly assembled orphans cry.
Don't give me none of your lip,
young man. He's been told, for the present
like Georgie and his plum-infested pie.
But listeners are more interested in rank-

ing hits, the lower the rank
the more they'll cheer (Bronx-style). Give some lip
to the arresting officer, get a lot of ouch,
if only in the wallet. No Xmas present,
this. You'll make your children cry
and it's once again *Bye, bye Miss American Pie,*

levied Chevy outranked by Honda mini-van. Lip
service never got you—ouch! That smarts! No time, no present
just a song to remember you, cry. The party when we kissed. You
    loved that pie.

Father's Day

The blue pen flows, the gospel radio brays.
This day is different from all other days.
No mass, no kaddish, everything's been said.
We'll plant a young tree with the kids instead,
right near the playground. *Now we say Amen.*
It's bluegrass now. A love we shared. I met
my fiddle hero at that festival,
your gig. He died just two years later: old,
a lifelong smoker. You were forty-five,
ate vegetarian and rode your bike.
Six-two, one hundred sixty pounds of brawn.
I wonder if they'll miss me when I'm gone—
the dobro twangs, the banjo taunts my ear,
the upright bass is—well, upright. Too clear.

Un-tombed

after Philip Larkin

Side by side, our faces blurred,
the couple that we were lay nightly.
Days uncounted, days too sure to end.

Three nights I've dreamed that you came back.
Three times my heart would start to settle in,
relieved. And then I'd wake up to the truth.

The beds where we lay together, queens
and doubles and occasional kings,
the basement bedroom in your parents' house

where we fought *sotto voce* every time—
another trip, another argument—
the tension snapped then eased up by the time

we passed the exit for Anne Arundel County.
No side-by-side monument will do for us.
You can't be set in stone—you're burned to ash.

I make my bed with our old flannel sheets,
aubergine, the color of dried blood,
worn even softer now, thin in places,

so many skins suspended in their folds.
I miss yours, blazing, irreplaceable.
The dreams don't bring your scent, your back,

your gentle but persistent snore.
The nights my coughing sent you to the couch
or you crept in wee-houring after work

are just as lost as the foldings-up and sighings
no effigy of coupledom can hold.
What will survive of us, my love?

Hundreds

after "Okónkolo" by Yosvany Terry

The güiro winds up slowly, ratcheting amperes
at the base of my spine. *I like the way you carry yourself.*
The cello plays and my hips start moving. You also liked
my opening line: *I really enjoy bowed bass
in a jazz setting.* Props from musician friends,
laughs for years. Before you proposed, you asked
the famous old guitarist how much to spend
on a ring: A hundred dollars? *A hundred dollars?!*
his reply. "A Hundred Dollars" you named the waltz
you wrote for the wedding. Dance of soprano sax,
trills and glissandi, a Raymond Scott riff—
I step a little lighter past Ferenga Funeral Home.

If you lived for five hundred years,
you asked me once, *what would you do with
your first hundred…your second…your third?*

We do not have the luxury of centuries—cadenzas,
shades of Casals—do I envy you because you left
before things could get any worse, left this world
I hate to love too much—broken triads, soaring unison,
widespread octaves? I too will surely leave
before I'm ready, even if I live to be a hundred.

Passacaglia

I still make inside jokes with you
even though you aren't here to get them
      strings wavering

The moon is a bright tired thing
everybody thinks they own
      night buzzes along

Salt water was your favorite
so cleansing, the passages
      crisp folds marked

Hold the bow lightly
technique finally perfected
      doors fly open

String Theory

I married a man who plays the barcarolle
or at least he did. In heaven now,
a great gig, on bass and drum and piano
the holy trinity of jazz, the beats
in my dreams on the edge of the seams.

How do you know when
it's time to restring the instrument
and start to play? When is it alright
to want again skin cradling skin,
the wrangle of sheets and comforter,
the pillows you keep smushing under your head?

Crossing the narrow chasm
from where we are to where you are no longer,
I nearly trip on my throat-lump,
tear-washed but not dissolving.

Snapshot: two on a porch waiting
for the father they can't live without.
It is late autumn, the holidays
and solstice weeks away.
A crescent moon trail forms
morning light at frost line.

O sky
whose beginning is nowhere
and whose end is all around us
you need no saucer, have no mate.

Positively East Fourth Street

After the poetry reading
I stop by Odd Fellows Ice Cream Co.
and ask the woman if I should get
buttermilk blueberry or lemon meringue pie
He bakes a whole pie to put in it,
she tells me reverently,
so I buy a cone.
It's gone before I get to the train.

Twenty years ago you played the internet cafe
across from the Hell's Angels on East Third.
Parking on that block was difficult
and the guy behind the counter was a jerk
but the jazz was good every night.

I always cry for you in the East Village.
I have for years now, even back when
it was only our marriage that had died.
Tonight, though, there are no tears
only ice cream and there is nothing
to compare with the absolute cleanliness
of the imaginary but this is close—
the whole pie in the ice cream—every bit
as tart and sweet as you expect.

Man and Widow

after Robert Lowell

Tamed by Milton, I lie alone in bed
Paradise Lost, the sonnets, all a muddle,
I can't remember anything I've read.
The *Areopagitica* blurs, befuddles.

You never lay beside me here. Our room,
the mattress that your mother handed down
before we wed, was in another home.
The kids and I moved here after you'd gone.

Those first few days as newlyweds we lay
with windows open, curtainless, the sounds
of the Greek festival two blocks away
washing through, bouncing off high ceilings.

The radio tonight: *Scheherazade*—
I dreamed we'd play it on our wedding night—
I drank too much. The hotel room you deemed,
barely used, *A waste.* Yes, you were right

about that and so many other things,
How practice is the key to art and love.
Our matching gold embellished Celtic rings
were no match for the wear of sorrow's rub.

When I was pregnant we bought a long pillow.
It flattened out a bit, we bought another
I hollowed with my body's growing billows.
Soon, we held pillows instead of each other.

Raised to be wife, I live alone, regret.
Now you're long gone, I live with this instead—
the spleen untempered, spinning up to fret,
my own tirades in waves upon my head.

Presidents' Day

"There was a lot of hair on the floor"
—from "Election '94" by Robert E. Bowen III

The cold is also beautiful, shrinking
my fingers, loosening my rings.
My right hand holds the pen
without slipping. Air circulates
in small spurts and drafts,
keeping me from dozing.

Elections were your thing,
your one published poem
about Republicans taking over
both houses in '94. *Everyone is an Asshole,*
capital "A," you wrote. You tried
to guide me away from absolutes.

In our first apartment we pledged
to clean the bathroom every two weeks.
Now I can't go two days without spraying
and scrubbing. The hair on the floor
is mostly our son's, long like yours
in your several hippie phases.

You lived to see a black man
in the White House, died before
his second term. Our son will be
a year shy of voting age this next election.
I wear rings only on my right hand,
the one I write with, farthest from my heart.

Silver Ring

I started as ore,
bright specks in rocky layers,
dull-colored, granular
and elusive. Miners went
down in the man carrier
and came back up
twelve hours later. Earthmovers
blasted up the rocks,
from rock to crushed ore.
Slurry in the muck bay,
rinsing, dredging,
and finally the furnace
burning off impurities.
I was lava-hot liquid,
formed into bars, bullion bought
and sold for market
value, spilled out in tickers
across the world, available online
to jewelers and to crafters.
A piece of me was hammered flat,
cut into strips, formed around
finger-shaped posts of various
sizes. Cut design, filigree, lace,
more heat to shape me. Set out
with others, tagged for sale.
You and your friend strolled
the main street of the town
at the mouth of Puget Sound.
It fit your finger perfectly then,
but now you can only wear it
on certain days. You fan your fingers,
forget they are not already

your mother's. Once, on vacation,
your daughter plays with me,
you flatten me with your foot
just enough that I am unwearable.
Later, visiting a friend in the country,
you sleep with her neighbor
who works in metal,
keeps me, coaxes me back
to my original shape, sends
me to you in the city,
parcel post.

Duration

The East River looks frozen, choked
eddies pulling in oppositions.
Cumulocirrus skies leak blue in spots.

You are not waiting at home
as you were so long, long ago,
solid point 'round which my currents churned.

Picking my way through stepped-on
frozen slush, I push my heart rate,
building stamina for the long haul.

How many more miles without you
or any other You? Families pass
on the promenade. The men

have all married younger wives.
The women are plush and beautiful,
their lips open delicately when kissed.

I have not forgotten how I had
to teach you softness, the relaxed tongue,
the release that made you squirm.

Spring is so late this year
we may never thaw again. Hard
to believe, harder to bend not break.

What the Living Say to the Dead

Our two young kids were monkey-scrambling
in my dream, and you, younger than ever, wanted me.
We roamed the stone buildings of some ivied campus,
working out our future, your apparent death behind us.
You would stay with me, with us, and all would be well.
Spring lilies were spreading in the pond, the first rowboats
tentatively nosing out onto the water. Shadows
alternated with dapples of sun, a buffet at midday,
cocktails and crudités at sunset.
At bedtime, we tucked ourselves in,
as we did so many times, sheets a-tangle,
when you were ours and I was yours
and the clock struck with no more than the usual
sense of dread. The problem with these dreams
is that I always awaken. You can't be too clear
when it comes to the dead, it seems, they have
so much trouble hearing you above
the din of everything they now know,
the music of the spheres and all the rockers
gone before their time, like you, the snowdrop cluster
of your love—surprise!—in the shade of a mossy old oak,
the sudden clearing where a lone fawn startles,
then turns to follow the doe it has so recently
emerged from, steaming and bloody and fierce,
hungering for balance, poised for the chase.

Riff – B

New York Nocturne

Insomnia is a luxury in the City That Never Sleeps,
since morning will come as it does, school bus
and sanitation truck huffing their way down
the street, construction starting outside your window
at eight a.m. sharp, per city ordinance, neighbors
shouting to each other over Alternate Side Parking.
Still, your body and mind conspire your overthrow
and there you are at four, getting up to pee
and coming back to screen the movie of your
greatest fears and insecurities, all the unsolvable
problems, a boulder that Sisyphus would've shrugged
and walked away from. You ask forgiveness of the dark,
though it is never completely dark, street lamps
and security lamps and house lights from houses
on top of each other, the lights strung along
the cables of the bridge like Christmas. They say
it's just hormonal, it happens as we age. Two hundred
years ago our ancestors were wakeful too, they had
"first sleep" and "second sleep" and a blank space
in-between when some of them lit lamps
put pen to paper. For you it recalls childhood,
those nights the shadows ghosted your ceiling,
noises creaked in the living room, and wide-eyed,
you trembling and clutching your new cloth puppet
till it was damp, sure you heard an intruder. Even then
you knew *If I should die before I wake* would come true
and, one day, the morning would renew itself
without benefit of you and all your silly worries.

What Are the Prospects?

Union Square Park swarms with students
and tourists, languages I can't identify,
families, mothers with toddlers
trailing sippy cups, men just off shift
lighting and then stomping cigarettes
before they descend to the train.
What are the prospects? The question I asked
every time I tried the online Tarot reading site,
hoping again and again for some ancient truth
to blow up like a billboard in living color,
explaining everything from the guy I wasn't hearing
from, to the poems I wasn't writing, to my kid
not getting out of bed for school. *What are
the prospects?* The blunt dull-dog persistence,
refusing to quit until I got an answer I could live with.
At the moment, the answer is curly kale
and whole wheat pita. I'm a pushover for fiber,
health kicks and promises, rooting
for moisture in a dressingless salad, settling
for the odd clump of feta, a lone pitted kalamata.
What are the prospects? Kaput, goosey gander
full-on shutdown, which we are not at liberty
to discuss at this time. They say spring
is coming, as it does, pushover that I am,
anticipating change, anticipating green pea shoots
and white asparagus, new lambs and all that bleating,
bleeding out and about in the world that remains
mostly fine, mostly inhabitable, mostly turning still.

Well Met

Imagine it's the museum where you run into him,
or getting drinks at the interval of a concert, a free
lecture or reception or under some storefront awning
waiting out a downpour, breathless. He's perfect:
handsome enough, age appropriate, healthy and ready
for love and not attached. You share the same credo:
carpe diem with a caveat, live every day, read *I and Thou*
through the lens of modern relationships. He catches your
eye and holds your gaze, takes your hand, you leap and WHAM!
wait—not that, a softer landing into a decent seat at the opera
and you see that he has already removed his hat
and stowed it safely beneath his seat. Breathe. No medic
necessary, no heavy drugs, prescription or otherwise. Push
the UP button on this one, check the YES box, run
towards not away and cancel the call for help. Ditto
panic, ditto vague dissatisfaction. Sit back, enjoy the show.

Supermooning

We craned to see the sumptuous supermoon
That drizzled on the foggy foreign sky.
It burned and sizzled on and on till noon.

You called from Massachusetts, much too soon—
You haven't just moved on. The spellbound try
And crane to see the scrumptious supermoon.

Emoji hearts don't hold the same balloon,
Confetti brings me down. Could that be why
It burned and sizzled on and on till noon

And stirred the frozen sea? I fought to tune
My inner carburetor's wiring guy.
We craned to see the unctuous supermoon

In separate states, in separate cloudstruck scenes.
I didn't press "send" at first, but by and by
The message burned and sizzled on till noon.

When suddenly my heart, that freeze-dried prune,
Began to thaw and soften. Mollified,
We craned to see. Rambunctious supermoon,
pray burn and sizzle on till long past noon.

Sestina d'Alba

Remember when we tasted our first kiss—
the way I loved the way you grabbed my arm
and, later, learned the talents of my mouth.
You do remember, right? The hotel room,
the king-sized bed (the first that we would lie
upon together), the two reunion drinks

you'd bought us that we didn't need? My drink
was gin and tonic, yours rum and Coke, your kiss
as sharp, as sweet. I cannot tell a lie.
When first I saw and stroked your wiry arms
I thought of bulk, of girth, of other rooms,
but soon forgot about those other mouths

I'd thought I couldn't live without. Your mouth
I barely felt as it trailed down—too much to drink,
too bent on pleasing you. The darkened room
whirred with possibility. The kiss
of morning sneaking in, we talked, your arm
around me, pillows stacked. How long did we lie

there? You told stories, I tried not to lie
when all I wanted was to feel your mouth
again where it had been while I was numb. Then, armed
with sunlight, bold, thirsty but not for drink,
you rose to leave, but turned for one last kiss
(the sound you made while kissing!) then left the room

to brave the jokes awaiting in your buddy's room,
and nap before you headed out to lie
on an airport bench, your flight delayed, our kisses
still lingering in the corners of your mouth.
Meanwhile, I dumped our flat, full un-drunk drinks
and groggily got dressed and packed. No alarm

was needed—how could I sleep? The arm-
chair had to be stripped of clothes, the room
scoured for left-behinds. Time for a cold drink—
iced coffee, some breakfast. On the road, lies
I told to calm myself leaked from my mouth:
I won't miss him or want another kiss.

We could have ended there, found other arms to lie
in. Instead, we've found another room. Your mouth's
found mine again. Let's drink: pour me a kiss.

Ruminalia

I pound my feet around the track, perforce,
I snack on berries, nuts, and chocolate
to leak endorphins, chemicals that late
were loosened by the parfait of your voice,

your surgeon's hands, your ice-blue eyes, the sweet
smell of your nape. Or, best, your mouth, which swerves
to square the brimming world along its curves,
the tongue that—never mind, I need relief!

Release this brain that ruminates to chew
its dry-grass cud. Let's meet by car, by bus—
You're there, I'm here. We're nowhere, meaning *us*—
that recipe yields more than two plus two.

Just tell me when and I'll make haste to graze
with you—a feast we'll both savor for days.

I take your T-shirt to bed again—

and by now it has almost lost its scent—
your scent, as when you were here and turned
towards the wall while I pressed my body
into your body and sighed, "You smell like candy"
into your t-shirted back. Yes, the smell is yours
the shirt warmed by your lean torso, tufted
and delicious. I've washed my clothes in your soap,
but that wasn't it—there must be something sweet your pores
pour forth. In three days you will be here and we will drink
from and with each other, sleep in close quarters,
naked, awake to heat and singing cells and slickness. But now,
too tired even to please myself, I breathe the shirt that covers
my pillow and dream—our *yes* and *yes* and *yes* opening and opening—

Creature Comfort

after Gerard Manley Hopkins

No. I won't despair this not-feast, not-you
not here, lazy lank and scruffed in my bed again
love-rub and slick-slide and just to feel
that mouth, to test-taste again your cock-plum—
no, lips, shifting beneath my lips, to hear
your growls and urgings and half-laugh, half-pant
when you're tingle-tipped and—*easy, easy*—
beg for me to stop. Remember, do you, how it looked?
Every man loves to see what sex blogs dub *pleading eye contact*.
I pled, I sought a service focal point—yes—yours,
every cell a-thrum with love, love, love the beat
and dying. What's to regret? That fought you sought
can suck a coupling dry with super-giving
your whole body, every cell, each molecule and then,
need-numbed, you cannot stop, for stop it never will,
now done, darkness, our wrestling wrenched (*you're God!*) your god.

Logistics for Thursday

Here's the deal: I'll buy
the first round of drinks, you cover the
appetizers and we'll go from there. Right
from the get-go we'll exchange books
and furtive, searching glances. All in
fun, of course—it's not as if the
future depends on any one evening, our best
behavior or the glue of a slim volume's bindings.
Is that your hand on my back as we saunter
to the park along the river? "Go on,"
I say, as you talk about the woods in Michigan
and I tell you again about Ohio at Easter,
all that green, the flowering trees, mornings
starting later than here on the coast. In
the middle of a sentence about the timing of sun-
rises and sunsets, you'll stop me with a kiss—Yes!—or
maybe my words will just be swallowed by the wind.

I am writing this with your pen—

which I forgot to give back, so flustered was I
by being near you the day I borrowed it. Last night,
while I was off kissing you, my son mussed
the covers of my bed, left a stray tube sock
like a careless lover. This morning I had to write
half of an essay for him on a "social problem."
He'd chosen Teen Drug Abuse because he's twelve
and not fifteen, the age at which his father started
smoking pot and didn't stop for twelve more years.
Clean when we met, he started up again towards
the end, when I was too much for him, and when
he quit it, he had to quit me, too. Then the world quit him,
the cruelest joke, and now the pen is good between
my fingers, smooth yet easy to grip without slipping.
Your thigh in jeans, the knee that still has feeling,
and the heart you've kept open—I imagine—just
enough to let mine rub against until it catches.

Midtown Valentine

On this day I will not choose between
parallel lines and perpendicular, between
sing and song, teeter and totter.
I will not make the call whether
to go north or south, take the direct route
or the long way home. This light,
wan blue sky and unforgiving sun,
the sound of crushing asphalt beneath
strong metal, the grinding of gears
you said we were feeling (hasp, rasp)
when we tried walking side by side.
There's a new pace in town, I hear.
I will not say you nay, though she
is half your age, the age of your own son
and you cannot bring yourself to kiss her
anywhere but the top of her auburn head.
You are no longer my problem, though how
to stay friends with you might be,
with your constant "We" this and "Us" that,
meaning You and Her. The ground shakes,
and three floors from the street I feel
the tremors of construction, which is really destruction,
a demolition of the heart of a neighborhood "in transition,"
translation: doing everything it can to bring
in the haves and push out the have-nots. Who will not say
the rents were unusual, the fire-escape lattice fair? Who won't notice
the crumble papered over, rot seeping slowly through?

Appetite

after William Carlos Williams

This is just to say I have eaten
all the chocolate chip cookies
I was saving for the children,
and now I am writing, one line
for every time I get the urge
to play Freecell solitaire
on my infernal mobile device.
One line, then one more for the itch
to grab something dark and sweet,
let my mouth have what it thinks
it needs. *Come on get higher,* the song goes,
reminding me that five years ago
my drug was a man—
his voice, his hands, his smell
so necessary that I wrote a poem
about that need, one that people read
and liked, because they too had endured
the craving for another body
in particular. "Caffeine and alcohol
are not a problem," I assured my doctor,
yet here I am again with an almond milk latte,
and tonight there will be cocktails
and gossip sure as it is Thursday.
It's all the same to the brain,
we're led to believe, liquid
or pill or powder, a person's touch
or sloughed-off cells, a game
of cards—even exercise
can hook you, apparently,
till you give your life—

Every breath you take—
we are still watching,
waiting, eager tongues
pushing through our teeth,
for one more dose,
so good and so bold.

Anatomical Life Drawing for the Illustrator

I

This introductory course in anatomy and life drawing focuses on the skeletal and muscular systems of the body in order to understand the human form, its proportions, contours, and characteristic periphery of movement.

After a drink or two, our old friendship,
the stories of our lives the past eight years
are mingled in a grand romantic script
complete with dinner, wine, dessert and—*Cheers!*—

a nightcap at the King Cole Bar. Perfection
the grand display of Parrish's nursery rhyme.
You point out lines and shadings, the inflection
of light and color. We kiss for the tenth time,

the artist's golds and blues collide and melt.
And then we're off—time for a new life study
a panoply of heat, contour, and movement.
Peel back the layers, and reveal the body.

What have we learned? Our parts become a whole
new form, combined, we barely can control.

II

This course extends the understanding of basic anatomy for the artists.
Students learn to artistically render the human form through the exploration of
composition, perspective, mood, and the effects of light.

Next time, you take me to the gallery.
I see your world: delicious and complex
enough to swallow pain and spit out glee.
The pictures crowd the walls, we crane our necks

to see the honorees above the throng.
Their colors swim on screens. I beg some air.
We grab a cab, your kisses stir a song
that softens, spins the night into a blur.

When morning filters light through naked trees
I wake and wonder what—your voice, your hands,
your mouth?—has rendered me so much at ease.
You've held me all night long. I turn and land,

a laughing composition on the floor.
You draw me back in bed with you for more.

III

Further study of the illustrative approach to life drawing, employing chiaroscuro and introducing color.

Maturity takes hold. We live our lives,
we have responsibilities. Let's sit
and drink, and talk awhile. It's Valentine's
Day, so I'm awash with mush. To wit:

the roses from a dear friend made me cry.
But you—oh, how that sweater holds your shape
with elegance, the green brings out your eyes!
This mix of dark and light is hard to take.

Resist the urge to storyboard in gray
the passion you won't let yourself indulge in.
You've pictured loving me and backed away—
it's not like choosing tempera or emulsion.

We drift homeward and pause to entertain
one kiss before we head off to our trains.

IV

*A study of the fashion approach to life drawing, involving increasingly complex
interactions of fashion concepts on the undraped figure. Expression, gesture, color,
and pattern are examined in relation to backgrounds.*

Fourth time around, we trade some memory scenes
that pop up from our youth in different cities.
The model who OD'd at seventeen
before you'd fucked or drawn her. Just as pretty,

my dreadlocked poet in vintage suits—he died,
I later learned, of AIDS. Boston, New York,
so much the same—wild parties we survived,
the scrapes that shaped us. Setting down your fork,

you reach out, almost touch me, stopping short.
I catch your eyes as they drift down from mine.
Your goodbye kiss so chaste—will we resort
to shaking hands when we link up next time?

Take my hand now, feel my blood warm your palm.
Come, take it. I can't hold this pose too long.

Curator

You acted like you owned them, all the books
in all the bookstores we wandered together, humming
titles and authors, dates of publication—
this is really rare—frank scent of must and dust,
the requisite cat and its litter box downstairs,
the workings of time on cardboard, cloth, and paper
and always that moment when my head would fuzz
like old-time teevee at close of broadcast day.

Why in all those trips through multicolored stacks
down narrow stairs, pulling me face-forward
into back issues of *World Book* and *The Century,*
did you not once take my hand? You ducked out
to grab *the best espresso* and pop right back
when all I wanted was to sit or, better,
to lie with you somewhere, heads propped on hands,
scanning the volumes of each other's faces.

How easy it would have been to kiss
on the freezing sidewalk that night, rush back
home, jazzed to start the reverential layer-peeling.
So many years your stories brimmed with women
who were not me. I counted myself lucky, all the work you took,
all you didn't do for them. Now I'd only ask you
to be there wearing a watch when I need the time,
to hold the door, safe entrance and even safer exit.

I cannot recall your mouth on any part of me,
but I remember your hands opening a book,
holding it up to turn page after brittle page
carefully with your long fingers, raising it up
above my head if I tried to peek or grab it,
making me wait until you were ready
to slowly reveal the riches,
such riches you had found for me.

I Saw the Light

There is nothing

        stirs the soul

like a mandolin

        opening into

full gospel

        bluegrass heaven

unless it is you

        singing "Shady Grove"

in my grandmother's

        living room

in 1988

        my uncle

on guitar

        your quavering naif baritone

your holey mustard-

        colored sweater

DON'T GIVE UP

the subway leaflet said, and we laughed
together at the thought that anyone
would call the number, expecting help
and hope. I'd call it now, I would,
if it could help me lose this itch
to press your doorbell, pick
the silly scab my heart has grown
since that night. Nights now,
and many mornings too,
I lie in bed thinking of your kisses,
wishing I had been bold enough
to grab the yellow paper
with its puzzling mix of symbols,
cross and heart and something sparkly,
keep it for this rainy day, the number
magic wiping clean my karma,
clearing the path for you
to find your way to me again.

Another Day

after Randall Jarrell

Moving from Cheer to Joy, from Joy to All,
I choose the brand
With less packaging, ingredients less likely to harm.
I add grain-free crackers, local greens, organic chicken,
Organic eggs, amaranth.
"Begin to be now," said William James,

"What you will be hereafter." I must begin
To be flatter of belly
And narrower of thigh, a fraction indivisible
By the lowest common denominator. In the name of health,
Everyone's selling
Kale smoothies, cayenne cleanses, grass-fed jerky.

When I was young and miserable and thin
I thought I was destined
To wear size six forever. How often did I undress
With someone then, how often lie alone imagining
I was being undressed?
I longed and longed till I was made of longing.

This new diet targets my demographic.
Oh, how I despise
Counting and measuring out discouraging portions
All the *no*-ing and the careful, careful shopping.
I crave compromise,
A plan that lets me sneak almond croissants.

At my slimmest I ate the most perfect pastries
From a tiny shop
Near Central Park. After therapy I'd get
My croissant and a large Sumatra with cream and sugar,
Careful not to drop
The phone no one called, walked to my favorite bench.

Dieting is common, but those croissants
Were extraordinary,
The filling not a paste but an almost-custard
Redolent of almonds. The shop is closed now—
Rising rent scary,
The tired owner sold her recipes to a neighbor.

Other middle-aged people annoy me,
Their huffings and umbrages,
Sun hats and hair dye and showy, pricey spectacles.
I am no exception, spending as much as anyone
To mask the damages.
It costs more and more each day just to go on.

I think of the two friends my age lost
Last year to cancer, one
Of the brain and one of the womanly organs,
One a three-month decline, the other a decade's battle,
Their daughter and sons
Bewildered, husbands devoted and diminished.

Yesterday, after fasting, I went to the doctor
Who put me to sleep
So he could peek inside and check for tumors.
He didn't find anything out of the ordinary,
Just told me to keep
Away from chocolate, caffeine, tomatoes, wine—

The few things that give pleasure to my days and nights.
I am not exceptional,
Staring at the mirror like a fogged effigy,
Unclear how one so young can look *like that,*
How one life can, after all,
Be so confused, so commonplace, so solitary.

Coda

The Argument

The failure of the flax crop is listed
as one of God's punishments.
The failure of our marriage
is listed as many kinds
of twine and rope. The kingdom
of heaven is not attainable
by means of a relationship.
The servants of the household
told their master about the weeds,
which are called *tares* in the King James.
I learned this because my family
were evangelical Lutherans, and you
did not because yours were liberal
Catholics. We found ourselves
together on valuable soil now
cleared, our children the best
fruits of the land.

***

I said that only to pique the imagination.
The paper shortage killed the experiment.
The blunt force trauma to lower extremities
killed you, which is why I can
never write about this, an encyclopedic
collection of information freezing
up the databases of my brain,
too many notes, too many words.
Not-so-brightly-colored is the tune
of the fall migration from Ohio.
July turned to August, we
made New York our home. The city
where our children were born,
the city that lost you.

***

As a rule, lazyjacks
are too slack, too unconcerned
with earning a living. To cast
anchor it is only necessary
to break one or two stops
in the sheet music—Finale
was your program, your sister
has it now, all your songs—
to offer what is precious to
those who are unable to keep it
safe and sound, it's all
out in the open though we
try to keep a lid on it.

***

Illustrations can help with understanding.
The guardian bears truth. Progression,
you showed me, was just chords
moving up the scale, chromatically
superior and cunning as it sounds.
O double-bind, O vogue in argument—
do you take translation from
divinities? Is it a sign
of continuance that our wretchedness
becomes our history?

***

After climbing awhile
beside the highway
we found a waterfall.

We always hiked too long,
too far into the woods—
we always made it back
before dark.

Your body lives
in my mind's meadow—
greening the hill,
spending the daylight
fast as it can.

ACKNOWLEDGEMENTS

Grateful acknowledgement goes to the editors of the following publications, in which some of these poems have appeared previously, sometimes in slightly different forms.

The Best American Poetry 2013: "I take your t-shirt to bed again"

Birmingham Poetry Review: "Anatomical Life Drawing for the Illustrator," "Creature Comfort," "Man and Widow."

Composing Poetry: A Guide to Writing Poems and Thinking Lyrically by Gerry LaFemina (Kendall Hunt, 2017): "Father's Day"

The Golden Shovel Anthology: New Poems Honoring Gwendolyn Brooks, ed. Peter Kahn, Ravi Shankar, and Patricia Smith (U of Arkansas P, 2017): "Logistics for Thursday"

The Goliad Review: "After Bathing I Smell Smoke," "Classic Vinyl" and "Good Housekeeping"

The Hopkins Review: "Un-Tombed"

Literary Matters: "The Miracles" and "Another Day"

Love Affairs at the Villa Nelle: 44 Poetic Temptations, ed. Marilyn L. Taylor and James Roberts (Kelsay Books, 2019): "Supermooning"

Michigan Quarterly Review: "SEA-BANDSTM"

Pine Hills Review: "What Are the Prospects?"

Post Road: "Curator" (nominated for Pushcart Prize)

SHIFT: A Journal of Literary Oddities: "I Saw the Light"

Starting Today: 100 Poems for Obama's First 100 Days, ed. Rachel Zucker and Arielle Greenberg (U Iowa P, 2010): "Audacious: An Acrostic"

SWWIM Every Day: "Duration"

Vitrine: a printed museum: "Sestina d'Alba," "I take your t-shirt to bed again," "Ruminalia"

WSQ: Women's Studies Quarterly: "M23"

Love and gratitude to my family and friends, especially Peg Bowen, David and Jennifer Lemmon, Judy Lemmon, Laura Heras, Jeana Baucant-Koon, Jackie Nowicki, and Rita Vasquez. In memoriam: Robert E. Bowen II, Robert E. Bowen III, and David T. Lemmon.

Thanks to John Gosslee and Andrew Sullivan of C&R Press, and to Brian Leung and Erik Rasmussen for the introduction.

Thanks to the Fashion Institute of Technology-SUNY for support in the writing and revision of these poems, and to Paragraph Workspace (aka The Cave of Making). Thanks, as well, to the Authors League Fund and the Poetry Foundation for sustenance in a time of great need.

For helping me keep to the path: Jean Amato, Isabella Bertoletti, Jessica Anya Blau, Naomi Gross, Julia Jacquette, Erica Moretti, Jada Schumacher, Amy Werbel, Lee Whiting.

For invaluable guidance with particular poems and the book as a whole: Barbara Hamby, Amy Holman, David Kirby, Alison Pelegrin, Elaine Sexton, Marcela Sulak, Kathrine Varnes.

Sustaining poetry pals and mentors: Kim Addonizio, Deborah Ager, Ned Balbo, Michele Battiste, Brendan Constantine, Erica Dawson, Sharon Dolin, Denise Duhamel, Moira Egan, Barbara Egel, BK Fischer, Sarah Freligh, Regan Good, Juliana Gray, Stacey Harwood, Gerry LaFemina, Dorothea Lasky, David Lehman, Phillis Levin, Heather McHugh, Donna Masini, Erika Meitner, Geoffrey Nutter, Nancy Pearson, Molly Peacock, Chelsea Rathburn, Jane Satterfield, Adam Vines, David Yezzi.

Note: The structure of the book was inspired by Leonard Bernstein's Prelude, Fugue and Riffs (1949) for solo clarinet and jazz ensemble.

C&R PRESS TITLES

NONFICTION

Women in the Literary Landscape by Doris Weatherford, et al
Credo: An Anthology of Manifestos & Sourcebook for Creative
Writing by Rita Banerjee and Diana Norma Szokolyai

FICTION

Made by Mary by Laura Catherine Brown
Ivy vs. Dogg by Brian Leung
While You Were Gone by Sybil Baker
Cloud Diary by Steve Mitchell
Spectrum by Martin Ott
That Man in Our Lives by Xu Xi

SHORT FICTION

Notes From the Mother Tongue by An Tran
The Protester Has Been Released by Janet Sarbanes

ESSAY AND CREATIVE NONFICTION

Immigration Essays by Sybil Baker
Je suis l'autre: Essays and Interrogations by Kristina Marie Darling
Death of Art by Chris Campanioni

POETRY

My Stunt Double by Travis Denton
Lessons in Camoflauge by Martin Ott
Dark Horse by Kristina Marie Darling
All My Heroes are Broke by Ariel Francisco
Holdfast by Christian Anton Gerard
Ex Domestica by E.G. Cunningham
Like Lesser Gods by Bruce McEver
Notes from the Negro Side of the Moon by Earl Braggs
Imagine Not Drowning by Kelli Allen
Notes to the Beloved by Michelle Bitting
Free Boat: Collected Lies and Love Poems by John Reed
Les Fauves by Barbara Crooker
Tall as You are Tall Between Them by Annie Christain
The Couple Who Fell to Earth by Michelle Bitting
Notes to the Beloved by Michelle Bitting